THE PINK BOUNCING BALL

THE PINK BOUNCING BALL

ALAN BALSAM

© 2017 Alan Balsam
All rights reserved.

ISBN: 0999275909
ISBN-13: 9780999275900
Library of Congress Control Number: 2017950861
CityscapeWorks, New York, NY

CONTENTS

Preface · vii
Introduction ·ix

Woodhaven and Ozone Park: Between the Highlands and the Bay · · · · · · · · · · · · · · · 1
Early History · 2
John R. Pitkin, the Father of East New York, New Lots, and Woodhaven · · · · · · · · · · 3
Ozone Park, the Work of Hitchcock and Denton · 4
In the Neighborhood in the Mid-1940s · 6
The Balsam Farm · 10
Introducing the Pink Bouncing Ball · 13
Children at Play · 16
The Ball and Its Domains in the Neighborhood · 17
At Rockaway Beach · 20
Slap Ball in the School Yard · 22
Dream Ball · 23
Stickball in Tudor Village Park · 28
Rafter Ball · 31
The Pink Bouncing Ball: An Appreciation · 34

About the Author · 35

PREFACE

This semi-allegorical writing features a history of the neighborhood in which I grew up, remembrances of it and my family in the 1940s, and adventures in childhood with the pink bouncing ball.

INTRODUCTION

Here are some tales from the neighborhood's history pages
Of a pink bouncing ball, a delight to people of all ages,
A paragon of play, with boundless energy,
A fabulous sphere, a great sensation,
A splendid gift for city kids, for happy times and recreation,
And countless adventures that banished humdrum from society.
In games with seemingly endless variety,
This favorite of an entire generation
Was limited only by a child's imagination.

But before the grand entrance of that vivacious ball
On the town stage in settings large and small,
Where the bouncer's adventures will soon unfold
And about which many a tale is told,
With elements woven as in a song, the introduction and refrain,
We consider the neighborhood in the 1940s, its principal domain,
An area that features a mixture of hill and plain.
We look beyond variation in terrain
To the history of the people in a particular place,
In a community that was unique, with much defining grace.

WOODHAVEN AND OZONE PARK: BETWEEN THE HIGHLANDS AND THE BAY

Woodhaven and Ozone Park are in the western part of the county of Queens,
And within that small region lies a great diversity of natural scenes.
In the north, the area is bounded by verdant hills,
Where in the quiet of night, the nightingale trills.
And in the south lies Jamaica Bay,
Where day and night, the cormorants play.

EARLY HISTORY

Dutch pioneers in the area were people of considerable means.
They were among the earliest settlers in the county of Queens.
In Upper Woodhaven, the landed gentry built homesteads that were safe and sound,
And as an added measure, there was always the family's trusty hound.
In Lower Woodhaven, near Jamaica Bay, their farms were found.
In the early days, the Dutch West India Company paid most of the bills;
All documents were prepared and signed with ink and quills.
Burghers, highly skilled in business, rarely saw empty tills.

Woodhaven and Ozone Park are united by a common history.
From the early days, Dutch settlements grew on an eastward trajectory,
From Manhattan to Brooklyn and then to Queens and Long Island.
The Dutch called the land along the Atlantic "Lange Eyelant."
In that era, the Woodhaven area was the site of homesteads and farms.
Work on the farm was labor-intensive and required strong legs and arms,
And essential for rainy and cold weather were work gloves and boots.
That history reminds us of our agricultural roots.

JOHN R. PITKIN, THE FATHER OF EAST NEW YORK, NEW LOTS, AND WOODHAVEN

In about 1840, Woodhaven, first called Woodville,
In a setting that was country-like and tranquil,
Became a municipality in New York state,
Thanks to the work of John R. Pitkin, first in dry goods then in real estate,
A founding father of the neighborhoods three.
To the door of success he certainly had the key.
A Connecticut Yankee, a real visionary,
His accomplishments were legendary.
He began town development in the early nineteenth century,
In the second decade,
Buying homesteads, farms, and land tracts just outside the city's border,
And then he had them surveyed.
Carving out lots from the land he bought,
Changing country chaos into urban order,
He planned how the towns would be designed.
Urban development requires much thought.
Economic slumps delayed some projects, but he would not be undermined.
He was active in philanthropy as well;
He understood that without social good, a town is merely a shell.
He sponsored trade schools for the poor and donated land to charity,
And those acts of kindness had a moral influence without parity.
They were a source of great civic pride
That was felt in the city, far and wide—
Gifts as bountiful as those from a plentiful horn—
So the name of the highway from East New York to Aqueduct and Jamaica Bay,
The "Old South Road," was changed to Pitkin Avenue, bearing his name even today.
And at the start of the twentieth century, facing that road, the Balsam Farm was born.

OZONE PARK, THE WORK OF HITCHCOCK AND DENTON

It was a time of building and development in New York City
In the inexorable march of history to new opportunity,
To the drumbeats of progress and innovation
When a landscape of vacant lands was made a community:
An important step forward for the entire nation.

Forty years after Woodhaven's founding,
Cool zephyrs from the north came bounding,
Sweeping south down the midlands and lowlands to the bay.
And a new day would be ushered in by the winds of change.
In 1881 houses arose in the Upper Woodhaven's flatland range.
On a large tract of land in the east, home to warbler, wren, and meadowlark,
One of many developments in the region whose name would end with the word "Park,"
Developers Benjamin Hitchcock and Charles Denton called it Ozone Park.
From 97th to 103rd Avenues and from 95th to 103rd Streets,
It was a sizable area, to say the least.
And for the time, building a community of that size was indeed a great feat.
From Woodhaven Boulevard (then 95th Street),
It was completely to the east.
In Pitkin's time the town of Woodhaven seemed like one large vacant lot;
The town was not a tale of what was, but mostly what was not.
Hitchcock, also a successful music publisher in Manhattan,
And Denton, his partner, were able to change that pattern.
In their neighborhoods the furniture you brought was mahogany, not rattan.
Their pitch to ordinary folks: "Open spaces, fresh air, and ownin' better than rentin',"
A big advantage compared with the crowded and congested Brooklyn.
Another important attraction to the city dweller was public transportation,
And indeed, very near the development was a railroad station.
Such was the real estate business of Hitchcock and Denton.
On the area they certainly left their stamp,
At the time of the birth of the incandescent lamp.

Woodhaven, at first an extension of Brooklyn, had been settled by Dutch pioneers,
Paving the way for those who followed and charted business pursuits and careers.
Then came Ozone Park, near isolated, easterly Idlewild.
One can say that Woodhaven was the father and Ozone Park the child,

The latter was built within Woodhaven as a residential enclave,
And settled by new European immigrants, who freedom and opportunity did crave.

IN THE NEIGHBORHOOD IN THE MID-1940S

At the time of Woodhaven's centennial, it was the dawn of a new day,
A time of great hope for the future and auspicious beginnings.
You could say that the odds were in your favor, and it was number one of nine innings.
A new generation, descendants of turn-of-the-century immigrants, started to find its way
On paths to success soon to be discovered, with great potential for winnings.
The dark clouds of the Great Depression and World War II had dispersed,
And in planning and building its future, our nation was completely immersed.
At the time, all was quiet in the streets of Woodhaven and Ozone Park
From the burst of the first rays of the dawn until the twilight surrendered to the dark.

Ozone Park was built near the end of the nineteenth century,
Which began as our fledgling country faced its "manifest destiny,"
Meeting the challenge of westward migration over lands of varied terrain,
So the limited area of original colonies our growing population would not constrain.
From the Atlantic shore, past the Appalachians, over the central plain,
Past the Rocky Mountains, all the way to the Pacific shore,
The westerly thrust was a source of strength and pride for the new nation.
The advent of the railroad helped stimulate westward migration.
In the early days, you could hear the loud rumblings of locomotives in the station.
First steam engines, then gasoline engines, and then electrical power came to the fore,
Bringing economic development, creating great opportunity,
Whose promise attracted the peoples of Central and Southern Europe and more.
And the people who settled in Ozone Park turned it into a community.

Starting in the twentieth century, after the new immigrants came,
The name Ozone Park took hold of most of Woodhaven town.
And after that, things were not the same,
But as with many a change, there was no reason to frown.
Semirural became suburban; newcomers' cultural diversity
Was a rather unique development in the history of New York City,
Which was growing rapidly on the wings of public transportation,
Whose effect was very much like the railroad's on the rest of the nation.

The pattern of Ozone Park and Woodhaven was grid-like, a logical way,
Streets ran north to south and avenues east to west,
So it was easy to find your destination, night or day,
And looking for a place was not a cumbersome quest.

Facing east, where the morning sun rose early in the day,
Beneath the path of snow geese and herons flying to Jamaica Bay,
We resided on 94th just south of 101st, a quiet street,
A place with many chances for play, that was great for children to meet.
Just about everything we could need was well within reach,
And a block away was Woodhaven Boulevard, the gateway to the beach,
A summer destination for family fun and relief from the heat of the day.
We felt lucky that the coast was just a stone's throw away.
In earlier times, 94th Street was called Walker Street,
And 101st Avenue, Broadway, a major road to Jamaica, the county seat.

The sidewalks were lined with lindens and maples,
The trees an attraction to the squirrel in the gray coat,
One of the area's animal staples,
Who like an actor onstage could certainly gloat
'Bout those tree acrobatics, such amazing feats.
For us kids, squirrel shows were wonderful treats—
Their talents the same on all trees, wide or narrow.
When they left, the birds came, flying straight as an arrow:
The starling, the robin, and the common house sparrow.

On both sides of the street, houses—two-family residences—
Faced one another, orderly, and without pretenses.
The work of multiple builders, around 1920, mostly clapboard but occasionally brick,
Varied in exterior design, cover, and color; blending them together was no easy trick.
Filling almost the entire rectangular lot,
Some houses were attached one to another, but others were not.
Heating was powered by coal, brought to the furnace by portable chute;
Coal was dispatched quickly by gravity, not slowly by force brute,
Thanks to that thoughtful chute invention;
Of its usefulness, there was no contention.

Laundry was unfurled in the backyard, on a line, attached with clothespins.
Occasionally, gusts of driving wind twirled those clothes, sending them into tailspins.

Landmarks included the Woodhaven Presbyterian Church, a corner highlight,
Built circa 1905 in the style of the Dutch Reformation,
A somber-looking architectural creation,
Yet, nonetheless, a very impressive sight,
Originally with a clapboard wood design and a very tall pyramidal steeple.
Its congregants included Upper Woodhaven and Brooklyn people.
Its red-brick façade would turn deep orange in twilight.

One block to the north, on Ninety-Fourth, stood P.S. 58,
A beacon of New York City public education.
A school'd been there since just before the Civil War divided our nation.
Most agreed that for learning skills by age five, there was no need to wait.
Studies included language, literature, history, and mathematics.
All that learning without diversion would certainly be a pity,
So there were regular recess times for play and children's antics,
Including the occasional singing or humming of a familiar ditty.
Built in 1859, a three-room wooden structure was like few others in the city,
And at first surrounded mostly by empty lots,
In an era of one-room schools, like the one near the family farm, P.S. 6 on Sitka Street,
Where a lone teacher taught older children and tots.
Children's education was a herculean feat
And the epitome of modernity to learn so much in one seat.

Before being demolished in the last decade of the century, when a new school was built;
It stood very straight, unlike the Pisa tower with its tilt.
It was a place where many neighborhood children were taught,
Inside, the three *R*s, outside, how a ball was caught.

Various commercial establishments stood on the avenue west and east.
The Ace Movie Theater, a treasure house of cinematic marvels, a child's delight,
Stood at 101st and Woodhaven Boulevard, a great location, in plain sight.
There you could see clear blue skies with eagles soaring, a visual feast,
And many dangers of the wild, with endless battles between man and beast.
The Cross-bay Movie Theater, an entertainment palace so grand,
That ticket holders who could not find a seat were willing to stand

For Roaring Twenties vaudeville shows and silent movies and a musical band,
And later, the talking film, the musical, and the rollicking cartoon,
With some entertaining comedian acting like a clever buffoon,
Singing songs with great charm, but often way out of tune,
Either early in the song—or later—but always easy to hear.
The theater was at Woodhaven and Rockaway Boulevards
In the former site of the Van Winklen Homestead,
Built at the turn of the 1600s—1700 the year,
When, to feed the family, you had to milk the cow and bake each loaf of bread.
It was built on what was at one time Everett Van Winklen's front and back yards,
Which for seventy-five years, were in the path of Dutch settlers' eastward migration,
By people with diverse interests and of varied background and station,
From Fort Amsterdam in Lower Manhattan to Hempstead.
And nearby was the Liberty Avenue elevated, a colossus of steel
On whose tracks the A train ran like the wind but kept an even keel.
That train would stop at Rockaway Boulevard station,
And take you to Brooklyn or Manhattan, whichever was your destination
A great pride to our nation, rising high in the air,
To get on that train, you paid a nickel for the fare,
And it would carry you far and wide
As if on eagles' wings to you could fly.
On the elevated train, you were almost in the sky,
And rain or shine it was great to be inside,
Indeed, it was a wonderful ride.

THE BALSAM FARM

My family had roots in Upper and Lower Woodhaven.
The north was suburban; the south, countrified, home of the common raven.
We resided in the north, and our dairy farm was in the south.
The Balsam Farm was an achievement spectacular,
A singular success—a big hit, as said in the vernacular.
During its beginnings, its reputation spread by word of mouth;
It was also a pillar of strength for the ages,
Worthy of note in the city's history pages.
Founded about 1900 by Isaac and Sarah Balsam, my grandparents, pioneers of the family.
Isaac, a lad of only eighteen, had emigrated from Poland (then Austria-Hungary).
Like many other immigrants, Isaac came with few material possessions;
He brought a Bible, a prayer book, a wealth of family traditions,
A will to succeed in the new world, no matter what the conditions,
And a flexible approach that included the ability to make concessions
In building a better life by finding a better way.
In those days, hard work was the main path to success, as it is today.
Coming to this land determined to realize the American Dream,
Isaac and Sarah were the principals, and they worked as a team.

I considered the Balsam Farm one of the great Wonders of the World.
It was home to three hundred cows,
Stately Holsteins that excelled in milk production.
The milk a product so loved that it required no introduction.

In a cow pasture with idyllic features,
Stood members of the herd of cows,
Undisturbed by neighborhood creatures,
Like the low-flying seagull or the barking beagle,
Placid domestic creatures, not known to get into rows.
You could recognize them easily, even from far away,
By the variegated patchwork of black and white on their backs,
Very distinct in the light of day.
Broadly proportioned they stood, with a demeanor regal,
Motionless in the meadow in a statuesque pose

As if they were glued to their tracks.
They appeared so unique from sturdy hoof to flattened nose
And used their tails to chase away any visiting fly
Or shook so briskly that the insect was happy to say good-bye
And then head directly toward the sky.

In that bucolic setting, they appeared so serene.
At the cold of winter, they never blinked an eye.
In the heat of summer, they never heaved a sigh.
They were permanent fixtures in the scene,
Like the sun beaming in the day and the moon shining at night.
And when nightfall gave way to early morning's glory,
Those central characters of the Balsam Farm story
Clearly outlined in the day's first light,
Standing like sentinels at their station,
Witnessing nature's daily cycle of creation,
They were steadfast in all weather conditions,
Proud guardians of the family's traditions.
And when fog arrived, bringing dense morning haze,
Their presence was felt, though they were out of sight,
Like an etching hidden on the back of a vase.

The farm had a bottling plant extraordinaire,
A dynamo of moving parts and energy,
A world of machines of great height, reached by a curving steel stair.
Milk was conveyed in a pipe and then out a spout into a bottle,
An engine that powered the process begun by a push on a throttle.
That scene for me evoked more interest and excitement than any building or bridge in the city.

It was number one in automation,
A "modern wonder of the world" is indeed an appropriate appellation.
In my view, its only serious competitor for that designation
Was the glorious A train, on the Liberty Avenue line,
Which was high on the list of favorites of mine.

There are many things you could say about the milk:
It had a great white appearance and a taste as smooth as silk,
Always interesting to view in a bottle of transparent glass

Emblazoned with the words "Balsam Farm" in bright red.
Milk from family-farm cows that were very well-bred,
As a product for consumption, had great appeal and class.
It could be greatly appreciated most any time of day
With or without cupcakes topped by icing in a rainbow of colors on the kitchen table,
And for kids you could truly say,
It made for a genuinely happy experience, and that is no fable.

INTRODUCING THE PINK BOUNCING BALL

In first grade, I was introduced to a family of words,
Soundalikes that rhymed with the word *all*;
Included among those was the word *ball*.
I thought of a ball as the oversized one with bright colors you take to the beach,
Which the wind often blows beyond your reach.
At that early age, I was not familiar with a hand-size pink ball,
But soon thereafter, as chance would have it, after a season of heavy snow,
When the starlings returned in spring from their warmer climes of fall,
Into my possession came such a ball, which I took wherever I'd go.

And I was a child of only five when I "met" this pink rubber ball,
A wonder of play that was destined to answer adventure's call,
Rivaling in interest a battalion of tin soldiers deployed on the living-room floor
Or a fleet of silver battleships not far away, near the entry door,
Bringing greater joy than multicolored marbles from the toy store,
Matching the thrill of watching baseball cards flipping to the ground,
Turning like wheels in the air without making a sound.
Such was the strong attraction of that small pink sphere,
Inspiring its owner to always keep it near,
Easily outdistancing a yo-yo in any competition—that and more.

About the size of an apple, the ball could fit in my side pocket.
Knowing it was there gave me a warm feeling inside.
It accompanied me on the sidewalks or the streets—just about anywhere outside.
It could fly from my hand and soar like a rocket
And at any moment at my behest,
And in its journey, travel far and wide,
Demonstrating spectacular prowess and zest.

On the day Isaac Newton sat under the tree,
Not by habit but purely out of whim,
An apple fell from a branch to the ground, but on the way took unexpected bounces,
One in a jarring fashion right off him,
Leaving him quite startled, interrupting his reverie,

But that was a great moment in history,
Leading to the discovery of gravity,
Which affected the pink ball, even though its weight was just a few ounces.
Gravity is the hidden force that affects any ball going up or down.
It also exerts the pull that makes a ball roll down the street.
On hilly terrain a bouncing ball can roll all over town.
The rolling ball, being hollow and light, meets less friction to slow it down,
And its journey may span a few inches to thousands of feet.

Any ball in the air has a pattern of rotation,
Depending on how it is thrown.
We generally refer to that as a *spin*.
A ball curving in its path can evoke great elation,
But to take an unexpected turn it is often prone,
And when it lands in the wrong place, like on your chin,
It may cause considerable consternation.
A ball may rotate forward or backward, or to one or another side,
When the ball hits a surface, the spin may be altered, changing the course of its ride.

Fling it up in the air, turn yourself around, and you can still catch it with your hand,
Throw it against a wall, and there is no telling where it will land,
Hurl it upward heading toward the sky
And above the treetops it will fly
And then fall to the ground but will not stop yet.
Bouncing in another direction, it continues to roll along the street, dry or wet,
And when it lands in a puddle,
There's no reason to fuss or get into a muddle;
Dry it fast, and for its next use you'll be all set.
Try to cast it straight down to the sidewalk fifty times,
And by the thirtieth bounce, the well-trained ball will seek out your hand,
And then, in your head, a winner's bell loudly chimes
To start celebrating and strike up the band.

On a concrete sidewalk or an asphalt-paved street,
The high bouncer was clearly the best choice for play.
For that purpose, when kids outside would meet,
There was never a bad time for a rubber-ball game, except on a rainy day.
A tennis ball had less bounce and when wet would get soggy and fray.

A softball or hardball struck with an impact too fierce, too dangerous for play.
Basketballs or volleyballs were in a different league
And were made for games so fast that they could lead to fatigue.
And to play you had to make a special effort for a place to seek,
As they required special courts not open every day in the week.

So, the pink bouncing ball, for many reasons, was the clear winner,
Its magic could carry the entire day until the arrival of twilight
(for when darkness descended, the ball would go out of sight).
Many kids were so engaged in play that they completely forgot dinner.

One day, I was heading outside with that marvel in hand,
But I was unprepared for what followed, truth to tell.
It was our landlady Jenny's cooking day, that I remember well.
The memory is so vivid because of an oppressive smell, the worst in the land,
That filled the air throughout the hall—
A powerful scent that could distract your attention and even make you fall.
As soon as I opened the door to descend the stair,
I caught a whiff of a very pungent odor of cheese.
It was so unpleasant that I could only hope to sneeze
Or, better yet, seek the relief of an outside breeze.
So, with no time to freeze, dally, or despair,
I hastened my steps into the fresh air.

It was a lovely spring day, in a sunny but rather cool month of May.
The lindens and the maples, with canopies of leaves, cast shadows at my feet.
Frequent zephyrs from the northern hills passed through en route to the bay,
Stirring the branches and causing their shadows to sway.
The weather experience was indeed a treat,
Though flannel shirt and corduroy pants were needed that day.

CHILDREN AT PLAY

After transferring the ball from one hand to another in one fell swoop,
I then threw it a few times at the house's front stoop.
It caught the risers in the brick stair.
Most often, it would hit a familiar pair
And bounce back straight into my grasp.
I held on tightly with my strong clasp.
I could grab the ball before it touched the ground,
Or I could snare it after it hit the street, on the rebound.
Once in a while, the ball would catch a corner of a stair,
And from there it could easily end up in a hedge, flower bed, or who knows where?
You could never get bored with toss-and-catch;
The game had a rhythm of its own that was hard to match.
It was the children's action equivalent of a game of solitaire.

That was a modest start for the ball, and it would soon see more exciting use;
The children of the neighborhood were outgoing, with nary a single recluse.
And in all seasons on any sunny day,
There was an opportunity to play,
And most would agree that for missing the chance, there was hardly a valid excuse.

THE BALL AND ITS DOMAINS IN THE NEIGHBORHOOD

Ninety-Fourth Street, where my family resided, was a quiet, tree-lined street,
A great place to play a game of catch and for neighborhood friends to meet.
In good weather, it was filled with children's laughter and glee
At play outside, a joyous sight for everyone to see.
In fun and games there always was a feeling of gaiety.
A bouncing ball required an active player to run after it,
To keep it from landing "wrong" after its fall.
The player had to be always ready to grab it and could never sit,
For often was there a second's warning of danger, or none at all.

There were places in the neighborhood that were out of bounds:
For one, you wouldn't want the ball near any acquisitive hounds.
We also had to watch for open rain drains near the curb,
Which the seeker of a lost ball could certainly disturb.

Experience said to never throw balls to a roof, pitched or flat;
With an inclined roof, in the drainage gutters, a ball could get caught.
For balls landing on flat roofs, we just threw up our hands and said, "That's that";
Retrieving a ball from any roof was way too danger-fraught.

Experience said to avoid heavy traffic that could part a ball from its master,
On thoroughfares like 101st Avenue or Woodhaven Boulevard.
Both had multiple hazards and promised certain disaster,
Unlike, for example, a playmate's fenced-in backyard.

Woodhaven Boulevard, gateway to movie theaters and sunny beaches,
For pedestrians was a busy roadway that lacked civility.
That came to mind each time I heard either car- or truck-brake screeches
That would disturb the neighborhood tranquility.
And in the games among girls and boys with the bouncing ball,
Even among kids with the most poise and agility,
Woodhaven meant peril for one and all.
The boulevard was all hustle and bustle—for residents, a harsh reality.

Woodhaven Presbyterian Church faced west, away from it,
To shut out noise—for practicality.
That orientation certainly for the worshippers was a better fit.
It was not a matter of Providence but architectural design strength.
There was one saving grace in the neighborhood: the street lots were long and narrow,
Keeping the busy highway at arm's length,
Preserving the quiet and creating a welcome refuge for the sparrow.

For the sake of noblesse oblige, certain places had no room at all
For the companionable pink bouncing ball
And its master's strong wish to heed the next adventure's call.
A good example was the family living room
With light sconces on the wall that "invited" a lob to dismiss momentary gloom.
Outdoors, one such place was the Woodhaven Presbyterian Church.
It presented an inviting large brick front on Ninety-Fourth Street, an expansive wall,
That, structurally superb, created a bounce-off that would make you lurch.
But I was told that the church was out of bounds for games one and all;
Anywhere around it was out, all the way to the curb,
As the sanctity of a place of worship, one should never disturb.
So the ecclesiastical domain could not be shared with the ball-spinner,
And that interdiction also reminds us: In battle between saint and sinner,
As in other human conflicts, among children there is no winner.

In most of the games you could play with the bouncer in pink,
The ball would move from hand to hand,
Often whizzing through air as fast as a wink
And in no time at all it would land.
The games were often played in a particular location
Outdoors: on sidewalks, streets, handball courts, or in the sand at the beach.
Their names were simple, too (no hardship for pronunciation).
The rules were straightforward and easy to teach.
They were of varied design and complexity,
Heightening interest for children of the city,
The merits of each game were easy to extol,
For most thrown balls came under reasonable control
And missing chances to play would be a great pity.

In slap ball and punchball, the ball was moved by hand,
As the player firmly on the ground would stand.
When hit, the ball took off in some direction, mostly not under control,
And could strike just about anything, which could take a dangerous toll.
It could fly high in the air or head down to the ground
Or head off somewhere else, there was no way of knowing.
But a clue to where it'd go was the creation of a sound.
An echoing tone meant a well-hit ball and that good hitting skill was showing.
The ball would then move in a forward direction
And to soar upward it had a predilection.
A ball that was grazed with the side of your hand would often move sideways,
And from the street it could easily enter one of the driveways.
On occasion, a game called for the use of a paddle or stick,
Which could send the ball farther than merely by throwing;
But hitting the ball with wood from a broom was no easy trick.

AT ROCKAWAY BEACH

On a sunny day in July, under a bright blue sky,
A family outing to the seashore promised to be a great sensation.
Rockaway Beach was the family's destination.
And on a day like that, no one would question why.
Preparations could be made almost in a blink;
You could bring most anything but, as they say, the kitchen sink.
My mom, Caroline, made sandwiches and packed the cooler with ice.
My brother, Joel, age twelve, took some magazines and comic books,
Easy reading for the summer outing, bought at a reasonable price,
With interesting adventure characters that attracted many a child's looks.
And I, age five, took a shovel and pail and a bouncer in pink.
My dad, Paul, drove the car along Cross-bay Boulevard, along the straightaway
Over Broad Channel and Jamaica Bay, directly to Rockaway.

It took no time to get settled at the beach
For everything you needed was in easy reach.
You could feel the cool ocean breeze
And hear a lady at water's edge, refusing to enter, saying she would freeze.
The blanket was spread over the sand, corners held down by this and that,
Including, at one corner, a wide-brimmed hat.
The umbrella was opened to bar the sun's intense rays;
The heat of the summer is felt most on such cloudless days.
And the blanket quickly filled up with people and things
And out came the pink ball, which soon into action would spring,
Flying in the air as if it had wings.

A sand mound was built with a ball roll around its edge;
It had the shape of a fountain.
The path around the mound was carved out like a ledge
Curving like on a road circling a mountain.
The path spiraled downward until it reached ground level, where it went out of sight,
Having entered an underground tunnel that meandered here and there,
And at any given time, the ball could be just about anywhere
Until it came to a shallow area near sand that was pristine white.

It would have been bad fortune for the tunnel to cave-in somewhere along the way
As it would have left me wondering about the ball's location.
At that point it would have to be left to one's imagination
And to rebuild the structure I could spend the rest of the day.

SLAP BALL IN THE SCHOOL YARD

In grade school, I was introduced to a game called slap ball,
An elementary children's variation of our national pastime, baseball,
But at the age five I had no understanding of the popular sport,
So learning slap ball helped me understand baseball, even though the field was short.
The school yard was very narrow as well,
So the scope of the game was limited, truth to tell.
There were three infielders, a pitcher, and a catcher, and one player in the outfield
Who, when the sun shone brightly, held up a hand his eyes to shield.
Whatever the shape of the yard, he stood in "centerfield."
He was master of that territory and to no one else would yield.
The pitcher would throw the ball with one bounce;
The "batter" with an open hand on the moving ball would pounce,
Trying to get the ball past the infielders, overhead or across the ground,
But it had to touch the ground before the outfielder caught it,
With bare hands, as with a rubber ball there was no need for a mitt.

Careful attention and a patient approach were considered skills most sound;
If you could accomplish that feat in the school yard,
You were as much of a hero as any player on a baseball card.
If you could not, then on the bench you would have to sit
But only as the limited space would permit.
In that small setting, punching the ball was not advisable,
You would propel it with too much energy, leading it astray
Beyond the field, which was not sizeable,
So to find the ball you could only pray,
That it did not wander to a place unknown
For to do that very thing it was surely prone.
That frequent nuisance was all due to our setting;
Against likely game delays it was not worth betting.
There was a fenced area beyond first base next to the school's side
That enclosed a below-ground level near the basement, I recall.
It was a right-field gap that opened wide,
So anything beyond first base would often mean a lost ball
And interrupt the game as the ball you had to retrieve—
An annoyance that for nonplayers was likely hard to conceive.

DREAM BALL

Something quite improbable, even close to impossible, in the domain of the real
Often happens easily in the world of the dream,
Where there are fewer distractions from a central theme.
And in a dream, most often, convention prevails, not the surreal.
Thus, no suspension of nature's laws is needed.
To the contrary, those are generally heeded.

In this dream, a race to Balsam Farm was planned between me and the ball.
It was an unusual challenge, as both were to arrive there together,
And there was no allowance with regard to vagaries of the weather.
And it was not possible to coordinate matters between parties with a telephone call.
For me to get there on foot would have been quite a hike,
So instead, I would choose a familiar path and ride my bike
Along quiet residential streets, on a route I very much did like,
A trip that usually took about a half hour, all in all.
But to throw a ball all that way would require the strength in Hercules's arm,
So the ball was left to its own devices in planning and making its trip to the farm,
A journey that would depend on various random events and forces.
In yesteryear it could hop on a wagon with a team of horses.
It could fly, bounce, or roll along any path it would choose,
Which was expected to be easy, as it was in its prime;
In the race, the ball was expected to win, not to lose,
Its main challenge was to arrive at the farm on time.
So as I approached the place, I expected the ball to sight,
Flying in the sky like a rocket,
From where it could descend and fall into my side pocket
Once I arrived but before from my bike I did alight.

Now, even in the context of a dream, that outcome seemed questionable,
As there were too many hurdles for the ball in such a race,
And combining the right moves for its success was quite implausible.
Steps had to be in proper sequence and timing right, to keep its pace,
To finish its journey to Pitkin Avenue and Eighty-Eighth Street—
So that the ball and I could meet
While I was still on the bicycle seat.

In addition, the ball had to obey the rules it followed in real time,
As there was no license afforded otherwise in a dream clime.
For example, it could not roll uphill;
It could not ignore gravity and in the air sit,
Nor like a flying saucer take off from a resting position, nor in any way move at will,
Without some force moving it.

Accomplishing such a goal would be a prodigious feat
That would certainly make you rise from your seat,
So my plan was to open a window of opportunity for the ball,
To help it meet its challenge's call,
Rather than relying on a voyage on wishes' wings
Or in the grasp of a large bird in flight that rarely sings
Or other equally unlikely things.
It is important to note that in doing so, I had to be discreet,
So I placed it on the landing in the hallway near the upstairs door
In an unnoticed corner on the floor,
So the initial step in the plan of action would be complete.
In addition, I left the downstairs door to the outside ajar,
And mindful that the distance from upstairs to downstairs was not very far,
I felt that having some slight advantage would be smart.
In that way at least, the ball would have a head start
To get itself onto the street
And thereby the outside world to meet.

As the dream began, much of the action was carried out by the ball,
Which was about to make its way down the stairs and through the hall.
It all unfolded as planned, without any noticeable commotion;
The upstairs door opened, and events were set in motion,
The ball got a nudge, rolled across the landing, and bounces down the stairs.
Unnoticed, it exited the house and onto the brick steps in front making its way,
Where it hit a corner and rose high in the air and then fell on the roof of a passing car
Heading south toward Liberty Avenue, three blocks' distance, I would say.
The event went completely undetected by the driver, who had not traveled far.
As the car was in motion, the ball quickly took flight
Toward the sky with the sun beaming bright.

As it happened on that day, a lady was airing a rug in front of her house,
Flailing it into the air with great energy as if there were some demon inside

That she had to remove, and she performed her work with vigor and pride.
And in a few moments, the rug and the ball would collide—
A sight to behold that would startle even an unshakable mouse,
An event that completely escaped her attention, as the rug was long and wide—
When the flying ball came in contact with the edge of the moving rug,
Witnessed by another neighbor who was holding a coffee mug,
And from there it sailed high in the air, to 103rd Avenue, a half block away.
After viewing that spectacle, in disbelief you could only shrug.
The ball struck the roof of an ice-cream truck heading in Woodhaven's direction,
which propelled it up in the air in the southbound lane, where it fell
Onto the roof of a school bus, at which point, truth to tell,
It idled a moment on that school-bus roof,
While from the rest of the world it was quite aloof,
As if unable to meet its destiny's call,

But this generalization was not true at all.
It was open to the elements, having absolutely no protection
From the strong winds of the north moving in a southeasterly direction.
The ball was lifted in flight high above the top of the tallest tree,
And it struck the façade of the Cross-bay Movie Theater, well above its marquis.
From there the ball traveled high and then headed down toward the elevated,
Where many passengers at Rockaway Boulevard stood for the train and waited.
That ball had risen above the el on Liberty at Woodhaven Boulevard, crossing
Rockaway Boulevard, reaching higher than possible through tossing.

Then came a train whizzing by from Lefferts Boulevard, and the ball bounced off its roof,
And it was launched like a rocket southward along Cross-bay Boulevard.
Pedestrians in the area to any goings on above were completely aloof.
It's not that they did not care; they were simply unaware,
For they rarely looked up, and the pink bouncer was one hundred feet in the air.
Then it came down to Cross-bay Boulevard and Pitkin Avenue, a familiar location;
It bounced off a garage in front of a corner house made of red brick,
Where resided Uncle Max and Aunt Rae and family in a house that was long and narrow
That received frequent visitations by the dove and the sparrow.
It was hard to follow a ball that quick.
Its maneuvers were like the sleight of hand in a magician's trick.
It then fell on the roof of a Balsam Farm milk truck that was heading to the farm.
Gently it landed as the heat of the summer made the air heavy and warm,
So it was as if by Providence that the ball really reached that location—

A happy occurrence that, even in a dream, is a source of great elation.
And for any beholder, the ball's appearance there was a true inspiration.

We turn next to my own trip to the farm that day,
Which began before the ball, heading into the unknown, started its own foray.
I selected the quieter residential streets on the north side,
On which it was much easier to ride.
I walked the bike past Liberty Avenue at the light, as that was the safest way.
I rode along 103rd Avenue until 86th Street and then turned toward the bay.
The south side of Liberty was quiet with no commercial routes intervening.
Looking at it and other neighborhood streets, I never felt they needed cleaning.
I coasted downhill until 133rd Avenue came into view;
The farm was close by; from experience I well knew.
To get there you had to ride past family-owned lots of sand;

They were rustic pieces of land over which the summer winds blew,
And trying to travel through those required a steady hand.

The ride along those sand lots was very challenging, and the wheels would spin.
The oiled sand would slow you down once you got in.
It was certainly not as easy as singing a song
And various things could go wrong.
The main problem for a bike rider, it was hard to get traction;
Low gear was frequently needed to move along
So that the bike and its rider could spring into action.
The wheels met friction in the varying elevations of sand, created by winds.
There was a tamped-down area that served as a road but was frequently in disarray
Due to cars driving across the lots, but that was no cause for dismay.
I passed a corner sign that asked the driver to yield.
I rode past Balsam Field, the Little League field,
Which most people did as a shortcut, and for no other reason.
I was on the Adelphi Paint Company's team in opening season
And on opening day, just before the umpire shouted, "Play ball," starting it all,
My father, the "Honorable Paul," threw out the first ball.

As it turned out, I had to focus on riding conditions,
But I was still curious about the whereabouts of the bouncing ball,
So I looked up in the air with the hope that it was about to fall.
And though it was not yet in sight, it would soon answer my wish's call.

Meanwhile, the ball sat comfortably on the roof of the Balsam Farm truck,
Traveling up Pitkin Avenue at a brisk rate of speed.
But as the truck approached Eighty-Eighth Street, it was blocked by a car that was stuck
And whose driver fussed over it as if it were a trusty fallen steed.
The car's motor would not start, so a tow was in need.
There was not enough room to pass, so the truck had to yield.
And as it came to a screeching halt, it caused the ball to take flight,
Assisted by a wind coming from the bay, blowing with all its might,
Turning the ball in the direction of Balsam Field.

When the bike became more steady, saving the rider from his plight,
Lo and behold, that ball high in the air came into sight.
In descent, it took a gentle curve that seemed just about right,
And while it was on the glide and I was still on my ride,
I made a quick turn to present my side pocket,
And the ball took the hint and fell right inside,
Fitting like a picture in a locket.
And after all that happened, I awoke from my dream!

STICKBALL IN TUDOR VILLAGE PARK

At a certain age, from slap ball and punchball you graduated;
On you would go to stickball, a game that was highly rated.
It was an important milestone that was rarely celebrated,
But that was a great change, one that should not be understated.
With a swing of a stick, a ball could be propelled high into the sky
And move nearly as fast as a swallow could fly,
A prospect that should not be underrated.
I was introduced to that game in Tudor Village Park,
Located not far from the Balsam Farm on Eighty-Eighth Street;
Any visit there I considered a treat.
With a few friends, I could play there almost till dark.

So up Pitkin Avenue I would walk in winter's cold or summer's heat
On the narrow southern shoulder of Old South Road,
And after wet weather, on the side of the street.
Near the farm I'd occasionally meet a jumping toad.
That friendly frog could serve as a teacher;
It required no trampoline to scale the heights.
A thoroughly vivacious and boisterous creature,
Its acrobatics rivaled those of squirrels on such nights.

And on Pitkin Avenue, you could watch its evening show under streetlights.
Walking up that city/country road, you would always move with traffic in your sights.
On a curving, hilly thoroughfare, you needed the eyes of a hawk,
And if you went by bike, up the avenue with it you'd walk
Up the road until 133rd Avenue, and then take a sharp left into the village;
The park stood on its distant end with interspersed lots empty of tillage.

Spring, summer, and fall were good for play activities in the park;
Winter, in contrast, was mostly excluded but not completely so.
When snow was on the ground, it was clearly a no,
But a cold, very clear day was always a go.
Such was the opinion of seasoned players, who were generally in the know.
On the short days of winter, play was interrupted by the early arrival of dark.

But sunny days with moderate temperatures were praised by the meadowlark.
And proximity to waters of Jamaica Bay was a warming factor in that section;
You might even see an errant gull riding breezes from that direction.
A trip to the park always possible for the optimist,
But likely rejected out of hand by the pessimist,
And clearly the odds for success in other seasons were certainly better.
Still, you could make do with flannel shirt and a heavy sweater.
Though cold weather certainly was unfavorable in the park,
You could stay there from the early morning daylight until dark.

During the day the village was generally quiet, and not much went on in the park—
That held true from sunrise until the arrival of the dark.
It was as though the park was merely an afterthought.
But it was the opportunity that kids sought.
It was the park of their dreams for children of the city.
There were handball courts and basketball courts that saw little use—not a pity,
For it was on the handball courts that games of stickball were played,
So when the courts were occupied, the game was delayed.

To play that game, two items were essential:
The pink bouncing ball and a broom stick.
The boisterous ball was always readily available;
For a stick, any idle sweeper offered great potential.
Among a bevy of brooms, you could take your pick,
And for the glory of the game, any choice was unassailable.
And with that the batter would try to hit the ball, no easy trick;
Timing and speed were important, and practice made your hitting slick.
And to any viewer of a ball soaring over the trees, it would not be clear from whence
It came a moment after you hit the ball, sending it sailing over the perimeter fence.

A rectangular strike zone was drawn on the white wall of the handball court.
It was prudent to swing at a ball in that zone; otherwise you would come up short.
The pitcher would throw the ball with a repertoire that varied,
Fastball, curve ball, slider, and combinations of those were what the wind carried.
A highly skilled pitcher could make the ball dance in the air
Although that was clearly exceedingly rare
And would add difficulty for a batter already somewhat harried.
But in the game, all that was considered fair.

There were usually four players—or only three in a pinch—
And starting the game was a cinch:
There was one batter, one pitcher, one in infield, and one in outfield.
But there were park benches in the middle of the playing field;
When they were occupied, the players to the people had to yield—
It was not as if players could give them a shield—
And the game could start only when the coast was clear,
Which was quite often, for with play in progress, people did not come near.

RAFTER BALL

Ever since the olden days, when people lived in huts,
The roofs over their heads needed supporting struts,
But in modern times, in most places, you almost never see rafters built into a ceiling,
Except in the belfries of churches, where bells are heard a-pealing.

In houses, rafters are seen in places like the attic and such.
Wood houses in New York were an important legacy of the Dutch.
But in older buildings, you can always see those flying wooden beams;
They are rustic, to be sure, which is not as rare as it seems.
On the farm, a walk through the upper level of a barn would reveal those supports,
Where occasionally a friendly mouse cavorts:
Flat rods of wood tracking at angles and along the horizontal plane.
They course in many different directions beneath the weather vane.

In summer, after the closing of the school season,
For children, camp in the mountains is an inviting destination;
It has many advocates, and each can give you more than one reason.
Attending summer camp became a growing trend for children throughout the nation.
Kids would have to temporarily uproot from family, friends, mutt, and kitty;
There was a world of discovery for children in the mountains, not far from the city,
Where you could see much farther than over the house windowsills
In the cool fresh air of the mountains of the Catskills.
There was much to be learned, including camping skills
And a broad range of sporting activities,
And you could develop various talents and proclivities.
(One young lad even learned how to whistle!)
On top of a cubby, the pink bouncer would sit
Before it was summoned into action, from which it would never quit.
On a postcard to home, the evening dining ticket, to wit:
"I'm OK. I went swimming today," was the happy news of that epistle.

So you would pack a duffel bag and a trunk
And put a label on each that read "Livingston Manor"
And go to camp, where each day they raised the "star-spangled banner."
When you arrived, you'd see your things were already sent to your bunk.

After a daylong bus trip up to the mountains,
Where hillside freshwater streams are nature's fountains,
Running down the mountain, glistening in the sunlight like a satin-blue shawl,
And where near the destination, along twisting dirt roads, low gear was needed for traction,
Finally, you arrived at the bunk, answering summer's invitation call,
And opened the trunk, and there in plain view was the pink bouncing ball,
A joy and comfort to one and all,
Ready to render service in the camp
And ready to spring into action
In all types of weather—hot, cold, dry, and damp.

But in many respects, the mountain terrain was unfavorable for that ball;
The camp was built on a hill, and there was little to stop it after its fall,
And the pink bouncer could easily go astray.
Yes, it could easily lose its way.
It could bounce off a rock, get lost under a bunk,
Or land in a puddle with a "splunk."
It could roll down the hill into thistle or even the lake:
Possibilities to be avoided at all costs, for goodness sake,
So it became a tradition that the ball was used in games inside the bunk.
There was no concern about fine china on the dining-room table or in a fancy store,
And there were few fragile objects vulnerable to an encounter with a clunk.
The interior was rustic throughout, and there were rafters galore
To be used in a game answering recreation's call.
It was given the name *rafter ball*.
You could toss the ball up in the air, and it could clear the rafter
Or bounce on it before returning to your hand, to be thrown up again thereafter.
A tossed ball would rarely land on a horizontal beam and there get stuck;
That would be a very exceptional event—perhaps a sign of good luck.
Even less likely, it could be caught by an errant nail or unseen hook,
But most often, it would bounce off the flat piece of wood
As chance would predict it should,
And it was so light that the beam hardly shook.
Occasionally, it would bounce more than once, twice, or thrice.
You would never know, as with the roll of the dice,
And you could score the game based upon the number of bounces the ball took.
This was a great indoor game, and it would gladden the children,

Who could perfect their skills in ball tossing.
During the day, during rest period between two and three,
The game would commence, and the bunk bristled with glee.
One or many could take part in this bouncing spree.

THE PINK BOUNCING BALL: AN APPRECIATION

And these are just some of the tales of that storied ball
That answered adventure's call
In winter, spring, summer, and fall,
In children's games leading to neighborhood explorations and sorties,
Bringing happiness and excitement to the generation of the forties.

We remember the ball in pink
That moved from hand to hand faster than a wink.
Heralded far and wide as a spectacular spinner,
Loved by the experienced player and the beginner,
In any game, it was clearly a winner.
It was a high flyer that could come from any side,
And sooner or later with something it would collide,
But nevertheless, always a source of great pride.

In the neighborhood, it was lifted by the highland breeze
On whose wings it could venture high in the air, far above the trees;
Under a bevy of high-flying cackling geese, it was completely at ease,
And fearless it was, even in the presence of a swarm of bees.

A favorite of a generation of city kids was the pink bouncing ball;
Its versatility was legendary; it was one of a kind.
When children went out to play, that ball was never left behind;
It was an inspiration to all.

Its feats were the central theme in many a story,
Leading neighborhood children on a path to glory!

ABOUT THE AUTHOR

Alan Balsam grew up in New York City in the 1940s, in Ozone Park, Queens. It was a period that may be called a "Great Historical Divide." Looking backward in the century, we faced three dark abysses: two world wars and the Great Depression in between. Looking forward, there was the hope of recovery and building for the future. His family and the place in which they lived also spanned important sociocultural and geographic divides. The family was descended from immigrants to this country from Eastern Europe at the beginning of the twentieth century. He lived on the north side of Ozone Park in a suburban area with his parents, Paul and Caroline Balsam, who were born in New York City in the first decade of the century, and brother Joel, but he spent a lot of time on the Balsams' family dairy farm in a semirural area on the south side near Jamaica Bay. As a child in that era, he adventured in New York's developing towns at a time when simple joys, such as the pink bouncing ball, brought children together and shaped their experience of childhood.

www.ingramcontent.com/pod-product-compliance
Lightning Source LLC
Chambersburg PA
CBHW081351040426
42450CB00015B/3392